Lafayette Post No. 140 Grand Army of the Republic

Ceremony of Flag Presentation to Columbia University of the City of New York

Lafayette Post No. 140 Grand Army of the Republic

Ceremony of Flag Presentation to Columbia University of the City of New York

ISBN/EAN: 9783337416973

Printed in Europe, USA, Canada, Australia, Japan

Cover: Foto ©Suzi / pixelio.de

More available books at **www.hansebooks.com**

Ceremony of Flag Presentation

TO

COLUMBIA UNIVERSITY

OF THE CITY OF NEW YORK

MAY SECOND, 1896, AND MAY SEVENTH, 1898

BY

LAFAYETTE POST, No. 140

DEPARTMENT OF NEW YORK

GRAND ARMY OF THE REPUBLIC

PRIVATELY PRINTED

BY LAFAYETTE POST

1899

Press of J. J. Little & Co.
Astor Place, New York.

June 1, 1894.

" Comrade Bach offered the following resolution, which was adopted :

"*Resolved :* That the Commander appoint a committee of five with power to arrange for presenting a stand of colors to Columbia College, provided that no expenditure therefor be made from the Post Fund, and the Commander is empowered to subsequently increase the committee to any number he may deem advisable. The Commander appointed as such committee Comrades Bach, Hendricks, Mills, Homer, and Greene."

THE COMMITTEE

JAMES B. BACH, *Chairman.*

RICHARD H. GREENE, *Secretary.*

E. A. WHITFIELD, *Treasurer.*

RICHARD W. MEADE, *Commander, ex officio.*
JOSIAH C. LONG, *Commander, ex officio.*
DANIEL BUTTERFIELD, *Commander, ex officio.*
WILBUR F. BROWN, *Adjutant, ex officio.*

ALLAN C. BAKEWELL
ALFRED C. BARNES
CHARLES A. BENTON
JAMES A. BLANCHARD
L. CURTIS BRACKETT
DANIEL BUTTERFIELD
WILLIAM S. COGSWELL
EUGENE H. CONKLIN
E. S. CONNOR
WILLIAM A. COPP
CHAUNCEY M. DEPEW
DANIEL T. EVERTS
FREDERIC GALLATIN
THEODORE K. GIBBS
EDMUND HENDRICKS

CHARLES F. HOMER
S. MERRITT HOOK
WASHINGTON L. JAQUES
JOSEPH J. LITTLE
FRANK C. LOVELAND
NELSON A. MILES
ABRAHAM G. MILLS
J. FRED. PIERSON
RASTUS S. RANSOM
WARREN E. SHEPARD
SAMUEL THOMAS
JERE. S. THOMPSON
BENJAMIN F. WATSON
ALEXANDER S. WEBB
DAVID F. WRIGHT

11

Executive Committee

JAMES B. BACH, *Chairman*.
RICHARD H. GREENE, *Secretary*.
E. A. WHITFIELD, *Treasurer*.
WILLIAM A. COPP.
EDMUND HENDRICKS.
CHARLES F. HOMER.
JOSEPH J. LITTLE.

Committee on Souvenir

JAMES A. BLANCHARD, *Chairman*.
WILBUR F. BROWN.
JOSEPH J. LITTLE.

Committee on Architectural Design and Inscription

ABRAHAM G. MILLS, *Chairman*.
DANIEL BUTTERFIELD.
CHARLES F. HOMER.

Committee on Ceremony of Dedication

DANIEL BUTTERFIELD, *Commander, Chairman*.
WILBUR F. BROWN, *Adjutant*.
WILLIAM A. COPP.
CHARLES F. HOMER.
ABRAHAM G. MILLS.

Extract from Minutes of Post

February 7, 1896.

" Chairman Bach of the Committee on Presentation of Flag to Columbia College made an exhaustive report, showing diagram of pedestal (marble), ornaments (bronze), and staff; the probable cost of which to be about $5,000. Comrades Mills, Homer, Greene, Kamping, Beyea, and Holly made remarks thereto; and on motion of Comrade Edgar, the following resolution was adopted, and the committee authorized to proceed with the plan :

"*Resolved:* That Lafayette Post formally accept the plan and scale of presentation of flag, staff, and base to Columbia College, as shown in this report, and in the drawing herewith, and empower the present committee to add to their number as they may deem expedient; and the committee are hereby empowered to obtain subscriptions for the needed amount from comrades of this Post, and also from friends of the Post or College."

·

NEW YORK, *February* 13, 1896.

MR. JAMES B. BACH, *Chairman.*

Dear Sir : Your letter of February 8th informing me of the action of Lafayette Post in determining to present to the College not only the garrison flag, but also the granite and bronze base and the flagstaff approved by our Committee on Buildings and Grounds, has given much pleasure to me and to the committee. In due course you will receive the official thanks of the trustees; but, in the meanwhile, I cannot forbear telling you, both on my own behalf and on behalf of the committee, that your action is doubly appreciated both for its generosity and also for its great patriotic significance.

Respectfully,

Seth Low,

President.

Extract from the Minutes

" At a meeting of the Trustees of Columbia College in the city of New York, held at the College on Monday, the 2d day of March, in the year of our Lord one thousand eight hundred and ninety-six, the following action was taken:

" *Resolved :* That the thanks of the trustees be tendered to Lafayette Post, G. A. R., for their generous proposal to present to the College not only a garrison flag, but also the granite and bronze base and flagstaff, the design for which was submitted to them by the Committee on Buildings and Grounds.

" A true copy.

Clerk."

F. V. Greene

NEW YORK, *March* 7, 1896.

COMMANDER RICHARD W. MEADE,
Lafayette Post, No. 140, *Department of New York,*
Grand Army of the Republic.

Sir : I have the honor on behalf of the officers of the Seventy-first Regiment to tender the services of this regiment as an escort to Lafayette Post in connection with the exercises at the new buildings of Columbia College on May 2d, 1896. I have written to President Low to the same effect, and I beg to say that the regiment will feel highly honored if the offer is accepted.

Respectfully yours,

F. V. Greene

Colonel.

HEADQUARTERS LAFAYETTE POST, NO. 140,
DEPARTMENT OF NEW YORK, G. A. R.,
MASONIC HALL, 6TH AVE. AND 23D STREET.

NEW YORK, *April* 27, 1896.

Special Order No. 1.

I. This Post will parade on May 2d, for the ceremonial of presentation of national flags to Columbia University on the occasion of the dedication ceremonies of the University site and buildings.

II. In view of the acceptance of a military escort (Seventy-first Regiment, N. G., S. N. Y.), the Post will be well represented on this occasion in the parade by the uniformed members only.

III. Assembly at 1.15 P.M. at the Forty-second Street ferry-house, North River, by comrades in the Post uniform, fatigue cap, white gloves, and black shoes.

IV. Badges that may be worn are limited to Grand Army badge, Lafayette Post badge, Medal of Honor for Gallantry, Army Corps badge, Army Society badge, Loyal Legion badge, and badges of the Society Cincinnati and Revolutionary Descendant societies.

25

V. Past officers and comrades desiring to parade with the colors will wear side arms.

VI. The Officer of the Guard will report to the Officer of the Day, at the place of assembly, with the colors of the Post, and receive a detail of twenty-five men for an additional guard to the colors on this special occasion.

VII. Past Commanders will take position on the staff of the Commander.

VIII. The adjutant will form the battalion in two companies, to be commanded by the Senior Vice-Commander and Junior Vice-Commander respectively. The colors will have position in the centre.

IX. Formation and programme have been arranged by agreement with the University authorities and the Colonel commanding the Seventy-first Regiment, in consistent keeping with the available space at the grounds and with the various exercises of the day, and the Commander confidently relies on a hearty coöperation and compliance with the regulations, which has always been the recognized spirit of the Post membership.

X. The Post, already historical, will add to its honorable record on this occasion, and the Grand Army will be benefited by the martial spirit and bearing of the comrades who will be conspicuous participants. Let every man be prompt and coöperative by strict attention and alert movement that the Post may hold on and add to its enviable reputation.

XI. For further information and instruction consult the programme herewith.

By order of

R.M. Meade

Official.   *Commander.*

WILBUR F. BROWN,

Adjutant.

PRESENTATION OF THE FLAG

On the day of the dedication of the site of Columbia
University, May 2, 1896, when the cornerstones of Physics
Building and Schermerhorn Hall were laid, Lafayette Post,
No. 140, Department of New York, Grand Army of the
Republic, presented two flags to the University—one a
large bunting or storm flag for daily flying, and the other
a silk one mounted on a portable staff with silver plate
suitably inscribed, for special occasions.

The Post, under command of Rear-Admiral Meade, assembled at the ferry-house at the foot of West Forty-
second Street, two hundred strong, in uniform, and were
mustered on board the boat "Annex" to receive the
Seventy-first Regiment, National Guard, which, under
command of Colonel Francis V. Greene, to the number
of six hundred, marched from their armory to the boat
to be an escort of honor. Proceeding up the river together, a landing was made at the Fort Lee ferry-house,
where the march began with the regiment in front, headed
by their band of sixty pieces, and, led by Colonel Greene
and staff, mounted to the new Columbian Heights.
Luncheon had been served to the regiment on the boat,
which had been provided by the Post. Reaching the

grounds, where were assembled thousands of citizens who
had gathered to be witnesses of the imposing ceremonies,
which had begun early in the day to last until its close,
the regiment formed in line to review the Post as it passed
to take its position in front of the vast assembly, near
to the speakers' stand, and around the temporary staff
erected to float the flag when it should be thrown to the
breeze to emphasize its grace and significance. In the
rear of the Post, after its position was arranged in good
military order, the regiment formed as a beautiful back-
ground to an inspiriting and imposing picture. Drawn
up in line of double ranks with correct alignment, the
men made a splendid appearance dressed as they were in
blue coats and white trousers, with their bristling arms
steadily held at carry, which appearance was assisted to
a brilliant degree by the " Field and Staff " superbly
mounted on animated steeds caparisoned with rich
accoutrements and with the brilliant uniforms and
white-plumed helmets of the commanding officers. It
was a spectacle never surpassed and rarely equalled on
any public occasion of ceremony in the history of the
city.

The order of presentation was unique and impressive.
The audience, large as it was, seemed spellbound and
was still, as if reverence for the flag had hushed all sound
that might disturb the harmony of the scene with the
importance of the occasion. Admiral Meade was superior
to himself in his address. His words gave expression to
the inspiration of his soul in language and substance far
beyond the most sanguine expectation, and his manly

form was a central figure in the picture that drew all eyes
upon it.

The resolutions of the Post which had moved the comrades to the adoption of the plan now begun, beautifully
engrossed, bound in white seal and clasped with a broad
tri-colored ribbon, were handed by Commander Meade to
President Low, who received them and stood in silence
while the flag, bent to the halyards, climbed aloft and
sprang forth with graceful waving in all its magnificent
glory. And then the people with one accord sent forth
a cheer of exultation and adoration that was almost tri-
umphant, and was as generous as it was voluntary and
unanimous.

The " Star Spangled Banner " was sung by all—faculty, trustees, students, audience, comrades, and soldiers
—a burst of song as if a nation was giving praise for the
Emblem of Liberty and Power.

President Low responded to the Admiral and accepted
the flags, evidently impressed with the richness of the gift
and the importance of its possession.

The ceremony over, the Post marched away in column,
and a few blocks below lined up on the avenue to present
arms to the Seventy-first as it marched by in review.
Behind us was the multitude cheering to the echo, and
the great tent was alive with thousands of people waving
hats and handkerchiefs, parasols, and canes, and the students throwing their mortar-boards in the air and flying
their gowns as signals of an animated and affectionate
farewell.

31

PROGRAMME

1. LAFAYETTE POST will assemble at the place and hour designated by Special Orders No. 1, and proceed with the Seventy-first Regiment by boat to One Hundred and Twenty-ninth Street.

Ununiformed members and those unavoidably delayed may proceed by Sixth or Ninth Avenue Elevated trains to One Hundred and Fourth Street, and thence by Amsterdam Avenue or Boulevard surface cars to the grounds at One Hundred and Sixteenth Street.

2. Under escort of the Seventy-first Regiment, N. G., N. Y., march will be made from One Hundred and Twenty-ninth Street to the University grounds, which will be reached by 2.45 P.M., at which hour President Low, trustees, and official guests will form at One Hundred and Sixteenth Street and Amsterdam Avenue.

3. On entering the grounds the military body will pass President Low and his guests, and take position in front of the Library Building, opposite the platform, flagstaff, arena and grand stands, and receive with customary

3   33

honors the President, trustees, and official guests, who will pass, on their way to the central platform, in front of the military.

4. At 3 P.M. prayer will be offered by the Rev. Edward B. Coe, during which the Post will stand at "parade rest."

5. After the address by the President of the University (during which the Post and troops will stand at attention), the following ritual will be observed, previous to the presentation address of the Commander:

Commander : Comrade Adjutant, for what purpose is the Post assembled ?

Adjutant : Commander, the foundation principles of the Grand Army of the Republic require that we promote and inculcate loyalty. In accord with this principle it is the custom of Lafayette Post to formally present to educational institutions the national flag, with a view to its being held in esteem and honor by the youth of ou country as an emblem of loyalty and patriotism. By resolution our Post unanimously tenders this great University of our city and State the national colors, together with a staff, a pedestal of granite and bronze, suitably inscribed and prepared. We are assembled for that purpose. I have the honor, sir, to hand you the resolutions properly attested.

Commander : Comrade Adjutant, it is well. Have all preparations been duly made ?

Adjutant : The flag is ready. The color guard has been duly detailed and instructed. The Post bugler is present for duty. The pedestal and base of granite and bronze with the staff await the completed preparations for their site and their dedication in the future.

Lafayette Post and the Flag

Commander : Comrade Adjutant, bring forward the guard and colors. Advance the bugler to his post. Let the flag be attached to the halyards, and hold all in readiness.

Here the adjutant will salute, issue the orders, and make the necessary preparation for the hoisting of the colors when the Commander makes the presentation address—at the close of which address he commands :

Commander : Comrade Adjutant, let the bugler sound " To the color," and while the flag is raised.

The guard having been specially detailed by the officer of the guard, viz. : four men (two sailors and two soldiers), will raise the colors—the bugler sounding " To the color " until the flag is in position at the peak, when he ceases playing, and the Commander, pointing to the flag, salutes the receiving authority.

The band of the Seventy-first Regiment will play " The Star Spangled Banner," and one stanza will be sung by the representatives of the Post and their friends, who will rise from their seats on the Lafayette Post stand.

STAR SPANGLED BANNER

O, thus be it ever when free men shall stand,
    Between their loved homes and the war's desolation,
Blessed with victory and peace may this heaven rescued land
    Praise the power that has made and preserved it a nation.
Then conquer we must, for our cause it is just,
And this be our motto, " In God is our trust,"
And the star spangled banner in triumph shall wave
O'er the land of the free and the home of the brave.

The adjutant, guard, and bugler will remain in their positions while the acceptance is taking place and until it is completed.

Immediately after the acceptance, President Low and Commander Meade will proceed together to the grand platform—the Post, preceded by the troops, will wheel into column and retire. After proceeding beyond the grounds, those of the parading comrades who so desire may return and take whatever vacant seats remain upon the platform which has been designated for use by the families of the members of the Post who have secured places.

By arrangement of the

GENERAL COMMITTEE.

Very truly yours,
R.W. Meade

SPEECH OF ADMIRAL MEADE

MAY 2D, 1896

(EXACTLY AS IT WAS DELIVERED)

PRESIDENT LOW :

As a soldier of the Grand Army of the Republic and
Commander of Lafayette Post, named for that chivalric
young Frenchman who crossed the seas to champion the
cause of freedom, I have been delegated by my comrades
to present to the President and Trustees of Columbia
University the flag of our country—to be hoisted at the
staff to be erected by Lafayette Post in front of the
Library Building, where, resting upon a granite and bronze
support, typical of the enduring nature of the principles
symbolized by the banner of the nation, there will be
found on the pedestal, in letters of bronze, the charge to
the students of Columbia to " love, cherish, and defend
it."

President Low, as I stand here in the presence of this
great gathering of men renowned in law, literature, art,
science, and commerce, I cannot help regretting that
instead of a professional man of the sword, our committee
did not select one of my comrades known to possess the

gift of eloquence. My words may seem feeble in comparison with those that might fall from the lips of one trained to the bar and schooled in all the arts and devices that move great bodies of men to uncontrollable emotion through the sublime gift of oratory. Yet I am consoled in the thought that the words I utter come from the very depths of my heart, and that what I say is the result of an experience as a practical defender of the honor of this flag we men of the sword hold so dear.

Why do soldiers and sailors of the Republic love their colors as men love life?

Why is this emblem of nationality so dear to the hearts of the soldiers and sailors of the Republic?

Because, sir, the flag is to us what the cross was to the Christian apostles, what the cross on the hilt of his sword was to the knightly crusader—the emblem of faith, confidence, love. The standard of a nation has ever been to men a most sacred thing, so sacred, indeed, that Holy Writ declares by the mouth of the great lawgiver (Numbers ii. 2): "And every man of the children of Israel shall pitch by his own standard with the ensign of their father's house"—so sacred that the Roman soldier was sworn upon his standard; and it was a common thing for the Roman general to cast the standard into the ranks of the enemy, knowing well that to every man of his legion that standard was so precious that the most desperate deeds of valor would be done to regain it.

And rivalling the ancients of the heroic age, tens of thousands of American soldiers and sailors have sealed their devotion to their colors with their life's blood on the battlefield, and the great loyal heart of this free people goes out in gratitude and veneration to them for it, and this great nation of seventy millions can forever be trusted to remember the men who uphold the honor of the Stars and Stripes; for loyalty to the colors, whether to victory or defeat, whether to life or unto death—these are the marks of the true believer. How great a crime then does that man commit who brings shame upon the flag, the emblem of his country! and how great is the glory of that man who reflects honor upon his flag, the symbol of the nation's honor!

One of the most beautiful legends in the history of Christianity is that which tells the story of Constantine's vision: how on the march to Rome, sore oppressed in mind with doubts and fears as to the issue of his bold adventure and half tempted to retrace his steps, suddenly at midday, above the splendor of the sun, he saw in the heavens a fiery cross, and beneath it in letters of flame the immortal legend:

BY THIS SIGN—CONQUER!

Who will gainsay the assertion that this glorious emblem of our nationality, the flag of the Union, is as much the sign of hope to us as the radiant vision was to the great Roman soldier? Look at it as it will presently kiss the winds with graceful folds and tell me if it be not the *one* true rallying mark for all honest hearts of whatever race or belief who own allegiance to this mighty Republic.

Look at its beautiful colors as they shine through murky clouds of this May day afternoon—the *white* symbolic of purity and honor, the *red* typical of the blood which has been shed and which will continue to be shed, if need be, in defence of the integrity and perpetuity of American institutions; and the *blue*, with its silvery stars, representing the great canopy of heaven under which the soldier of the Republic on the land toils on the weary march or bivouacs in the silence of the night, or the sailor on the broad expanse of ocean keeps his weary watch and vigil, that the citizens of the Republic may rest secure, while over all He who watches over the destinies of this mighty nation of freemen, He in whose kindly providence our forefathers implicitly trusted, neither slumbers nor sleeps.

And under this immortal banner men of all shades of political opinion, of all forms of religious belief, can rally for the eternal principles of right, justice, and liberty under law. Loyalty to the Stars and Stripes—loyalty to the flag of the nation—that is the creed of the American. Perish the thought that there may be found dissenters to this creed north, south, east, or west.

Our flag, sir, is the flag of peace—it stands for peace, and not for war. Wherever it goes it carries encouragement and cheer to races of men less favored than ourselves. It is everywhere a harbinger of hope to the oppressed.

It stands for liberty unsullied by wanton license—for freedom to worship God " without let or hindrance "— for the equality of all men before the law—for the greatest good to the greatest number.

It is the flag of peace, progress, and prosperity—it is not the flag of selfish aggrandizement. It has been the symbol in battle of the justice of its cause, for I dare to assert in the presence of this great gathering that Americans have never waged unjust wars and that, God helping them, they never will. It is the flag that in the most terrible civil war of modern times stood always for morality, not rapine; mercy and not ruthlessness; magnanimity and not revenge—oh, sir, the flag of a benign Providence itself, for it symbolizes justice, mercy, and unity under the stars of heaven.

Then, sir, if my words be true, be diligent in season and out of season to charge your youth who enter these venerated halls of learning, to love, cherish, and defend it.

THE COLORS ACCEPTED

President Low then accepted the colors in this eloquent speech:

COMMANDER AND
COMRADES OF LAFAYETTE POST, G. A. R.:

On behalf of Columbia University, I accept with gratitude and pleasure the flag you have presented to us. That you propose to add to your gift a permanent base and staff for the flag, is welcome, but well I know that in your thoughts, as in ours, the flag is the principal thing. In the defence of this flag and for what it means, sons of Harvard, of Yale, of Princeton, of Columbia, and of all the sisterhood of American colleges have " thrown away their lives like a flower." In the name of the men of King's College who fought for the independence of the colonies, and who did so much to establish the government of these United States ; in the name of the men of Columbia College who in the War of 1812 and in the Mexican War fought under this flag in the country's quarrel; and in the name of the men of Columbia University who fought, as you fought, in the war for the preservation of the Union, and who helped to bring

47

unscathed out of the storm of the war this glorious flag.
I pledge you for this University that we shall " love,
cherish, and defend it." As we shall be ready, God
helping us, to die for it in case of need, so I trust we shall
be ready to live for it, striving always to make the country over which it floats ever worthier to be loved.

> Long as thine art shall love true love,
>   Long as thy science truth shall know,
> Long as thine eagle harms no dove,
>   Long as thy law by law shall grow,
> Long as thy God is God above,
>   Thy brother every man below—
> So long, dear land of all my love,
>   Thy name shall shine, thy fame shall grow.

MY DEAR MR. BACH:

Please accept my thanks for your very cordial letter of
yesterday, expressing the satisfaction of Lafayette Post
with the ceremonial of Saturday afternoon. By common
consent, the presence of the Post and of the Seventy-first
Regiment acting as their escort, added importantly to
the scenic effect of the occasion, and the patriotic episode
of the presentation of the flag evidently touched every
heart.   I am thoroughly delighted that the Post is satis-
fied with the outcome of my suggestion to them that the
presentation of the flag should be identified with the occu-
pancy of our new site.   It would have been altogether
impossible for us, in our present location, to have given
to the event any such color or character as it had on
Saturday.

Immediately after the ceremony, I ventured to express
my congratulations personally to the Commander of the
Post upon the admirable address in which he presented
the flag.   It gives me pleasure to say that my own favor-
able opinion has been confirmed by the observation of

4   49

many others. Please express my thanks and the thanks
of the trustees to your associates of the committee and
to the comrades of the Post for all that they added to
the success of Saturday's ceremonials. I am little at a
loss to know how to acknowledge the presence of the
regiment otherwise than through you, inasmuch as they
were present as the escort of the Post. I trust, however,
that it may be permitted me, through you, to express to
Colonel Greene and the members of the regiment our
sincere appreciation of their participation in the interesting event.

I am, dear sir,

Very respectfully,

President.

Mr. James B. Bach,
Chairman of the Committee of Lafayette Post,
29 Broadway, New York.

NEW YORK, *May* 6, 1896.

JAMES B. BACH, ESQ.,

    29 *Broadway, City.*

Dear Sir: Mr. W. H. H. Beebe has referred to me your letter of May 4th, and I take pleasure in sending you herewith proofs of all the addresses of the afternoon ceremonies of the dedication. I regret that I cannot provide you with a sufficient number of copies of the programme to be bound in your book, but if half a dozen copies will be of any service I shall be glad to send them to you.

Permit me to take this opportunity to express the gratification of the trustees at the part taken by Lafayette Post on this occasion. Their presence gave to the day a national and patriotic significance which it would not otherwise have had, and added immensely to the dignity and effect of the occasion as well as to the general interest. The gift of the Post is appreciated by the trustees not only on account of its intrinsic value, but of its significance and its example.

      Very respectfully yours,

51

May 7, 1896.

Mr. John B. Pine,
　　67 *Wall Street, New York.*

Dear Sir : The proofs of speeches, etc., came to hand very acceptably. I will be glad to receive the half dozen programmes offered by you. We appreciate the kind words of your letter, and we certainly have reason to feel gratified that Lafayette Post was permitted to take so prominent a part in the ceremonies on the afternoon of the second instant.

Permit me to express the belief that in the future, as well as in the past, to be a student of Columbia College means also to be a lover of country and our flag.

With one so honored by all in command at the University, and so efficient board of trustees, the progress of the University to the highest mark desired cannot but be sure.

Very respectfully,

Jas. B. Bach

Chairman of Committee of Lafayette Post.

HON. SETH LOW, *President,*
    Columbia University, New York.

Dear Sir : Your favor of the 5th instant is one that I will have the greatest pleasure in presenting to the Post at its next meeting.

Our circular sent to our comrades when the presentation was decided upon will show that we appreciated the honor at that time, as we all do now, that we were permitted to participate in the afternoon ceremonies of the University.

Our Commander shall know of your compliment. I have had a copy of your letter prepared to send to Colonel Francis V. Greene, commanding Seventy-first Regiment, which will go with one from me as chairman of committee, thanking him, as you desire, for the authorities of the University, as well as conveying the thanks and appreciation of our committee for the honorary escort by his command on the 2d instant.

Respectfully,

Jas. B. Bach

Chairman of Committee.

Col. F. V. Greene,

Commanding 71st Regiment, N. G., N. Y.

Dear Sir: It is with great pleasure that I forward to you a copy of letter from the Hon. Seth Low, President, addressed to the chairman of the Committee of Lafayette Post on Presentation of Colors to Columbia University, wherein due acknowledgment is made of the presence and services of the Seventy-first Regiment at the dedication of the University grounds on Saturday, May 2d. At Mr. Low's request I cordially thank you and the regiment for honoring the occasion. The appearance of your regiment produced a fine effect in every way, and it certainly was a happy thought that brought your offer to Lafayette Post to be their escort.

Please also convey to your officers and men the sincere thanks of Lafayette Post committee for the honor done us, and we desire to express our admiration of, and esteem for, yourself, officers, and your men. We thoroughly appreciate the great courtesy which prompted you to such an offer, a compliment which will not be forgotten.

Our committee send our best wishes for you all.

Yours respectfully,

Jas. B. Back

Chairman of Committee of Lafayette Post
on Presentation of Colors, etc.

NEW YORK, *May* 11, 1896.

JAS. B. BACH, Esq.,
Chairman of Committee, etc.,
Lafayette Post, G. A. R.

Dear Sir: I have the honor to acknowledge the receipt
of your letter of May 7th, enclosing one of May 5th from
President Low, in regard to the participation of the regiment in the ceremonies connected with the dedication of
the grounds of Columbia University on May 2d. I beg
to thank you, and, through you, the Commander and
comrades of Lafayette Post, as well as President Low,
for your kind words, which will be communicated to the
regiment in orders ; and also to assure you that every
member of the regiment was proud to take part in this
historic event, and specially pleased to witness those most
interesting and impressive ceremonies.

Assuring you of our high regard and respect for Lafayette Post, and thanking you for the privilege of being
thus associated with you, I remain,

Very respectfully yours,

F. V. Greene

Colonel.

RESOLUTIONS

adopted by the Post, June 5, 1896, and bound in seal-
skin, which were presented to Colonel Francis V. Greene,
January 1, 1897.

" *Whereas :* The formal presentation of the national
colors to Columbia University by Lafayette Post, May 2,
1896, on the occasion of the dedication of the grounds and
the laying of the cornerstone of the great educational
structure to be reared, to be followed by the gift of a
granite base with bronze ornaments with a seventy-foot
shaft, was a movement full of patriotic sentiment and
loyal teaching ; and

" *Whereas :* The escort to the Post by the Seventy-first
Regiment, National Guard, voluntarily offered, gave evi-
dence of the loyalty of that noble body of troops to all
that the flag represents; therefore it is

" *Resolved :* That the warmest praise be accorded to
Colonel Francis V. Greene and his associate officers for
the quick perception of a patriotic purpose made manifest
by the tender of the escort of the regiment of their
command in a proper military display on so worthy an
occasion.

" *Resolved:* That much is due to the rank and file for the ready response and full representation of the regiment and the martial bearing under orders.

" *Resolved:* That whatever applause was bestowed or praise given over the spectacle as the colors floated to the air amid the cheers of voice and notes of trumpet, should be shared with the escort, who added to the scene by their splendid appearance.

" *Resolved:* That the thanks of Lafayette Post be unanimously given to Colonel Greene, officers, and men, for their magnanimous courtesy so generously expressed by full ranks and military etiquette, and that they be suitably expressed over the signature of the Commander of the Post, attested in proper form and presented.

" Signed:

R.M. Meade

Commander.

"*Attest:*
" WILBUR F. BROWN,
Adjutant."

DEDICATION AND PRESENTATION OF
PEDESTAL AND STAFF

MAY 7, 1898

BASE OF PEDESTAL

LOVE
CHERISH
DEFEND
IT

NORTH PANEL

SOUTH PANEL

-ANNO DOMINI-

-MDCCCXCVI-

WEST PANEL

-PRESENTED TO-

-COLUMBIA-UNIVERSITY-
BY
-LAFAYETTE-POST-

-NO 140 DEPT OF NY-

-GRAND ARMY OF THE REPUBLIC-

EAST PANEL

PRESIDENT'S ROOM, *April* 20, 1898.

My dear Mr. Bach: I am in receipt of your kind letter of yesterday. I suggest that the members of your Post rendezvous in Schermerhorn Hall, which is the new building at right angles to Amsterdam Avenue. The approach is by the front steps and to the right of the Library. The main hall of this building is very wide and well suited for the formation of a procession, and in immediate connection with it is a large lecture room with seats, where the veterans can remain in comfort until the time comes to march.

I am inquiring whether the students' band can play " The Star Spangled Banner." If so, that will be, I think, a pleasing feature of the ceremonies. I propose to invite the trustees, the faculty, and the students to be present. On Saturday afternoon, in the spring, we may not have a very large crowd; but there will be enough, I am sure, to give dignity and interest to the occasion.

Thanking you for your good offices,

I am, respectfully,

President.

MR. JAMES B. BACH, *Chairman*,
    29 *Broadway, New York.*

LAFAYETTE POST
No. 140
DEPARTMENT OF NEW YORK.
G. A. R.

ORDER OF EXERCISES

AT DEDICATION AND PRESENTATION OF PEDESTAL AND FLAGSTAFF
TO COLUMBIA UNIVERSITY BY LAFAYETTE POST, NO. 140,
DEPARTMENT OF NEW YORK, GRAND ARMY OF THE REPUBLIC,
MAY 7, 1898

President Low, with the officials and students of the
University, will assemble at Schermerhorn Hall at 3.30
P.M., and, being duly formed, will precede and escort
Lafayette Post to the flagstaff and pedestal.

1 SONG AND CHORUS—"America."

2 G. A. R. CEREMONIES OF RAISING THE FLAG—
Lafayette Post.

3 SONG—" The Star Spangled Banner."

4 PRAYER OF THE CEREMONIES—By Chaplain Wood
of the Post.

5 GRAND ARMY CEREMONIES OF DEDICATION—
Lafayette Post.

6 PRESENTATION—By Major-General Daniel Butterfield, Commander of Lafayette Post.

7 SONG—" Three Cheers for the Red, White, and
Blue."

8 ACCEPTANCE BY PRESIDENT LOW.

9 SONG—" Praise God from Whom All Blessings Flow."

10 BENEDICTION—* Rev. Morgan Dix of the Trustees of Columbia University.

The procession of officers and trustees of Columbia moved from the Library ; Lafayette Post, with music and colors, moved from Schermerhorn Hall at 3.30, and formed at the flagstaff. General Butterfield, Post Commander, and President Low leading, followed by the trustees and faculty of Columbia College; students, moving from University Hall, being formed on the left.

SONG—" America."

The Commander, General Butterfield, orders :

" Adjutant, you will detail a guard of honor."

(Adjutant selects and calls his guard.)

(Adjutant.) " Commander, the guard is present."

(Commander.) " Officer of the day, you will direct the officer of the guard to station this detail."

(Commander.) " Holy Scripture saith : ' The Lord gave the word; great was the army of those that published it.' Ps. lxviii. 11.

" ' Declare ye among the nations, and publish, and set up a standard.' Jer. l. 2.

" ' In the name of our God we will set up our banners.' Ps. xx. 5.

---

* Acting for Rev. George R. Van De Water, the chaplain of the University, who is absent with his regiment in the field.

" Officer of the day, you will order the guard of honor to raise the flag."

(Officer of the day.) " Officer of the guard, let the flag be raised."

(FLAG IS RAISED.)

(Music.) " The Star Spangled Banner." Sung by Post and students.

(Commander.) " The chaplain will now offer the prayer of dedication. (Parade rest !")

(Chaplain.) " We pray Thee to make our memories steadfast, that we may never forget the generous sacrifices made for our country. May the graves of our heroes be the altars of our grateful and reverential patriotism.

" And now, O God, bless Thou this memorial.

" Bless it, O God, in honor of mothers who bade their sons do brave deeds.

" In honor of wives who wept for husbands who would never come back again.

" In honor of children whose heritage is their fallen fathers' heroic name.

" In honor of men and women who ministered to the hurt and dying.

" But chiefly, O God, in honor of men who counted not their lives dear when their country needed them ; of those alike who sleep beside the dust of their kindred, or under the salt sea, or in nameless graves, where only Thine angels stand sentinels till the reveille of the resurrection morning.

" Protect it, and let it endure, and unto the last generation may its influence be for the education of the citizen, for the honor of civil life, for the advancement of the nation, for the blessedness of humanity, and for the furtherance of Thy holy kingdom.

" Hear us, O God. We ask it in the name of Him who made proof of the dignity and who consecrated the power of sacrifices in His blessed life and death, even in the name of Jesus Christ, the Great Captain of our salvation. Amen !"

(Comrades.) " Amen."

(Commander Butterfield.) " Attention !

" In behalf of Lafayette Post, Department of New York, Grand Army of the Republic, I now dedicate this standard and pedestal, knowing it will keep bright memories of those who in the navy guarded our inland seas and ocean coasts, and fell in defence of the flag. I dedicate it, knowing it will recall memories of those who in the army fought for our hillsides and valleys and plains, and fell in defence of the flag. I dedicate it, assured that it will bring heartfelt gratitude to those who on land and on sea fought for the Union, and fell in defence of the flag ; who on land and on sea, fighting for their country, and for the law and the Constitution, fell in defence of the flag; also gratitude to those who are now in arms at their country's call, and who stand ready with their lives, their fortunes, and their sacred honor to do their duty."

(Commander.) " Post, attention !"

ADDRESS OF PRESENTATION

By GENERAL BUTTERFIELD

Mr. President Low:

Our services of dedication are ended. Holding in my hand a list of the gallant sons of Columbia who in years past, from its foundation in 1754 down to the commencement of the existing war in April, 1898, beginning with Thomas Marston, a graduate of 1758, your first class, who was a member of the Revolutionary Committee of 1775, and including such distinguished alumni of Columbia as John Parke Custis; Harman Rutgers, of the Continental army, killed in the battle of Long Island 1776; Major-General Alexander Hamilton, of the United States army, who was upon the staff of General Washington ; Jacob Morris, of 1775, an aide-de-camp to General Greene ; Ogden Hoffman, of 1812, midshipman in the United States navy ; a De Peyster, captain of the United States army; a Kearney, colonel of dragoons and brigadier-general in the army, and governor of Vera Cruz, and of the City of Mexico during the war of 1848 ; another Kearney, the famous brave and gallant " Phil " Kearney, a major-general, killed at Chantilly, at the age of forty-seven, in 1862 ; the brave General Ellis, killed at Gettys-

burg, and the noble Richard Tilden Auchmuty, breveted
for gallantry at Gettysburg ; F. Augustus Schermerhorn,
breveted for gallantry at Five Forks, who gave his splendid yacht to the government a few days since; General
Stewart L. Woodford, now on his way to us from Spain;
General Henry E. Davies, of the class of '57, who won his
stars as a major-general at the point of his sword in the
war for the Union ; Henry Ketteltas, of the same class,
breveted for gallantry at Shiloh, Chickamauga, and
Mission Ridge ; Alfred T. Mahan, who went from here to
graduate at the Naval Academy in '59, and so through
the long list in the staff and other departments.

Time does not permit to name them all, although in-
cluded with the list are members of our Post, and the
names of such distinguished families as the Jays, the
Morrises, the Kings, and members of your faculty now
with you, the surgeon-general of the army and others.
These names are reminders that it needs not this flag,
it needs not eloquence nor words of patriotism, for the
purpose of inculcating in the sons of Columbia a spirit
of devotion to flag and country. That seed has been
well planted here, and will continue in the future, as in
the past, to bring forth its fruits. I recall with pleasure
and pride your own eloquent words upon the historic
field of Gettysburg, and your glorious tribute to the
gallant Fourteenth Regiment of Brooklyn, to-day again
in the field at its country's call. I fully realize what
effect the words and example of your administration of
Columbia will be ; it suffices to give you for Columbia
this tribute from our Post of veterans; may it perform

the double duty of saying to you, to the young men assembled here, and to those who will come in the future, that our veterans, and the veterans of the Grand Army of the Republic, appreciate the service of Columbia's sons for that flag, and have full confidence that their glorious service in the past will always be repeated in the future.

In the name of my comrades of Lafayette Post, No. 140, Department of New York, Grand Army of the Republic, representing soldiers and sailors who defended the integrity and authority of the nation in the past; in the names of my comrades who in the present are again showing their loyalty and devotion to the flag and country, I present to you this pedestal and staff dedicated to the purposes set forth in the address of our late Commander and comrade, Admiral Meade, when the flag, glorious emblem of our nationality, was presented two years since. With those ceremonies we may now recall the words and promise of our then Commander, the gallant and lamented Meade.

You will find in imperishable bronze the words so impressively spoken on these grounds to you by Admiral Meade: " Love, cherish, and defend it." You will also find the emblem of our order, whose history (yet unwritten) I trust some day may be, replete as it is with the grandest spirit and example of fraternity, charity, and loyalty of a noble character, in the service and the money it has given from the generosity of our comrades to comrades and their families in distress.

Accept it, sir, with our trust that the historic loyalty

and devotion of Columbia to our country and flag, its prompt response to every call and requirement therefor, will continue to add to the rolls of honor to be emblazoned upon the walls of your splendid and historical institution of learning. It is yours, the gift of our comrades to Columbia.

Accept it, sir, and may blessings and prosperity ever rest upon you and upon Columbia in future as in the past while you adhere always to the principles and spirit it illustrates and calls forth—

AND MAY GOD BLESS COLUMBIA.

Song—" Three Cheers for the Red, White, and Blue."

LAFAYETTE POST

N⁰ 140   G.A.R.

DEP'NT OF   NEW YORK

ORGANIZED 1880

ACCEPTANCE OF PEDESTAL AND STAFF

By PRESIDENT LOW

GEN. BUTTERFIELD, COMMANDER, AND

COMRADES OF LAFAYETTE POST:

When Lafayette Post, only two years ago, at the dedication of this site, gave to this University the national colors, and made the promise, so generously fulfilled to-day, of this lofty and noble staff from which our country's flag now proudly flies, it did not seem likely that within so short a time the United States would be at war. The flag that we then received at your hands was the more precious to us, nevertheless, because, in your presence, we could not forget that our flag is what it is by reason of the self-sacrifices that have been freely made for its sake; and because we rejoice to receive the flag from men who had themselves fought for what it stands for, under its inspiring folds. It was not, therefore, in careless mood, but most reverently and earnestly, that, in receiving the flag at your hands, the men of Columbia University promised to " love, cherish, and defend it." More quickly, I dare say, than any of us then thought probable, the time has come when you may judge in

87

what spirit the Columbia of to-day is likely to redeem that pledge. As you have yourself pointed out, sir, we would be false to all our traditions were we to be backward in responding to the call of the country at such a time as this. But there has been no hesitation. The University has already surrendered four of its officers to the public service, and has charged me to see that not one of them suffers by reason of his absence at his country's call. The captain of the University crew has handed in his resignation that he might go out with the naval militia, and the students have accepted, uncomplainingly, this heavy blow to an interest that is very dear to their hearts. Scarcely a regiment or a naval battalion has volunteered from these parts that has not counted in its ranks one or more of our students; and others stand ready to follow when the call comes. I do not know how many have gone in all; but enough, certainly, to bring home to those who are left a realizing sense af the paramount claims of the country, and to assure you that your trust in the men of Columbia has not been misplaced. I must be permitted, also, to refer with pride and gratification, as the President of the University, to the patriotic act of Mr. F. Augustus Schermerhorn, both an alumnus and a trustee, who in the present emergency has freely given his yacht to the government, as in the days of '61-'65 he offered his life. He was breveted, as you have said, sir, for gallant conduct at the battle of Five Forks; and he is breveted now again, by the public voice, as a citizen worthy of high honor because he has chosen to give this vessel to the government at a time when he might have sold the yacht to it at a high price. These are the things that show Columbia's spirit; and they show, I am glad to believe, the same lofty patriotism that has animated the men of Columbia from the beginning.

But if this flag and staff make an especial appeal to our patriotism, that is only a part of the service they will do for us. They will inspire the scholar at his desk and the graduate in his office no less than the volunteer on land and sea. The country needs men willing to die for it, but it also needs men willing to live for it. The country has need of sound learning, of fearless investigation, of patient study and reflection, no less than of the service that can be rendered in the day of battle. No hope can lie in the atmosphere of this University, no ambition can be cherished here, that will not gather fresh inspiration from the sight of this staff and banner with their silent but eloquent summons to the constant service of country and of mankind. Was there ever a flag before in the world's long history that stood for so wide a sympathy with the downtrodden and the oppressed? that meant so much of help and hope to the weak and the discouraged? Nor can I doubt that, as we look upon our country's flag, the feeling of gratitude will be deepened in us all for the blessings of civil liberty and for the opportunities for study and for usefulness that abound in the wide land over which float so caressingly the Stars and Stripes. I am confident, therefore, that all our life in the University will be the deeper, the broader, and the richer because of this flag and the staff that you have given to us. If this be so, what more can you ask? You have added to our life as a university some touch of the earnestness that strengthens purpose; some breath of the sympathy that constrains to an unselfish life; some sense of the loyalty that elevates and ennobles all who submit themselves to its influence. For all this we thank you; and again we pledge ourselves to you who have given to us this staff and this beautiful and precious flag, the flag of our beloved country, that in peace and in war, in war and in peace, we will " love, cherish, and defend it."

Hymn—" Praise God from Whom All Blessings Flow."

Benediction by Chaplain Wood of Lafayette Post.

PRESIDENT'S ROOM, *May* 9, 1898.

My dear General Butterfield : I write just a line to tell you how much we all enjoyed the ceremony of Saturday afternoon. Every one who took part in it thought it a most impressive occasion. I need not say to you that we are very proud of our staff and flag, and that the University feels very closely united in interest with Lafayette Post of the Grand Army of the Republic.

Thanking you and the Post for all you have done for us, I am,

Respectfully,

President.

GEN. DANIEL BUTTERFIELD,
    616 *Fifth Avenue, New York.*

DESCRIPTION OF PEDESTAL AND STAFF

The flagstaff is a single stick of Oregon pine, 18 in. diameter at butt and 7 in. diameter at top, surmounted with a gilt eagle with wings spread.

The butt of the staff is set in a cast-iron base 3 ft. by 3 ft. by 16 in. high and 2 in. thick, which in turn is set in a solid mass of concrete 9 ft. by 9 ft. by 9 ft.

The pedestal, of pink Tennessee marble, rests on a granite base octagonal in shape, 9 ft. 8 in. smallest diameter by 9 in. thick. The pedestal itself, also octagonal in shape, is in three courses, 18 in., 22 in., and 8 in., respectively, thick, or 4 ft. above the base.

The middle course is panelled on four sides to receive the bronze design and lettering as elsewhere shown by photographic reproductions.

The pedestal is surmounted with bronze work of a highly ornamental character 4 ft. in height.

SPECIFICATION

As finally approved by the committee on behalf of the Post for the work to be done in the erection and completion of the foundations, base, and flagpole to be erected at Columbia College, Morningside Heights, New York City, for Lafayette Post, No. 140, Department of New York, Grand Army of the Republic, in accordance with the plans prepared by and under the general superintendence of

McKIM, MEAD & WHITE, *Architects,*
160 FIFTH AVENUE, NEW YORK CITY.

July, 1897.

Excavations   Do all necessary excavations as shown by the plans and sections and to the dimensions marked thereon, and remove all superfluous earth, etc.

Level off and ram the bottom to a true surface.

Concrete   Lay the concrete footings as shown by the drawings; the concrete to be composed in the proportion of one of Dyckerhoff Portland cement to two of sand, to four of broken stone.

The cement to be of the best quality Dyckerhoff Portland cement, and to stand the tests used by the Columbia College authorities in testing all cements used in the construction of their buildings.

The sand to be of the best quality Cow Bay sand, clean, sharp grit, free from salt, loam, or other deleterious matter, and to be properly screened before mixing the cement.

The stone to be of sound granite, gneiss, or trap-rock, screened free of dirt and rotten stone, and washed if required and directed before using; to be of the size of hens' eggs, or that which will go through a two-inch mesh screen. All to be carefully measured in barrels and mixed in proper plank boxes prepared for the purpose.

The cement and sand to be mixed dry and spread over the broken stone, then a sufficient quantity of clean water is to be lightly sprinkled on, and the whole turned over and mixed uniformly until fit to be laid in the foundations, as will be approved by the architects.

Lay in the foundations in layers of about eight inches in thickness, and level off and ram on top of each layer until the moisture comes on the surface.

Lay so as to break bond if jointed, and properly rough up clean and moisten the surfaces of each course before laying the next course.

After the first course of concrete is laid, the cast-iron shoe plate will be set to receive the pole, and a twenty-four inch square mold will be set on top of shoe to form hollow square in concrete to receive shaft.

All concrete to be laid as rapidly as practicable.

Level off on top of beds for first course of granite steps.

After the pole has been set in place fill in the space between the pole and the face of concrete with liquid Portland cement, tamped down until filled solid to the top of the concrete.

Filling in Fill in around the concrete foundations on the outside with clean coarse gravel and earth, thoroughly and firmly rammed to the level of under side of first course of granite steps.

Provide and set a cast-iron shoe plate as per detail, to receive the butt of flagpole, to be a good, sound, clean casting, of tough gray iron, out of wind and free from all defects, of the dimen- *Cast-iron* sions and thicknesses shown on the details, to be painted *Shoe Plate* one coat before setting of Detroit Graphite paint for iron and another coat after setting, to be set on the top of concrete in Portland cement, true and level.

The granite to be used in the first course in ground will be of the best quality Pink Milford from the quarries of Norcross Brothers or the Pink Milford Granite Company.

Cut Granite and Marble Work The marble to be used to be Pink Knoxville.

The granite and marble to be selected from the best stock the quarries produce, and must be entirely free from vents, shakes, streaks, and any or all other defects, and be of good and even color. No patched or filled stones will be accepted. The granite and marble to be cut so as to lie on their natural quarry bed when set, and must hold the full sections and lengths and be bonded as called for by the drawings.

All beds, builds, and joints will be fine point work, full, true, square, level, and plumb for $\frac{1}{8}$ inch joints ; no slack beds or joints will be allowed.

The face work will be of the best quality ten cut work ; the moldings, arrises, angles, etc., to be all cut sharp and clean.

The tops of steps to be weathered.

The raised faces of panels on the sides of die of pedestal will be polished in the most thorough manner ; no acid must be used.

Cut all dowel, cramp, and lewis holes that may be necessary, and provide all copper dowels and cramps.

Cut the hole through the centre of pedestal, die and capping to permit the passage of the flagpole through same into the foundation, to be six inches larger in diameter than the base of the pole.

Set the first course—granite—in four stones as shown ; the second course—marble—or step course with molded face and nosings in four stones, the molded panelled die of pedestal—marble—in one stone, and the capping—marble—of same in one stone.

All to be set in H. H. Meier & Co.'s " Puzzolan " cement and sand mortar, mixed in the proportion of one of cement to three of sand.

The putty for pointing the joints to be of Meier's cement lime putty and Rockaway sand, mixed in the proportions of one of cement, six of putty, and eight of white sand, the cement and sand to be mixed thoroughly together dry, water added gradually in mixing to prevent the flooding of the cement away. The joints will be raked out carefully and trimmed off, and be pointed with the above mortar in the neatest manner.

The granite and marble work will be cleaned off and washed down with clean water, wire brushes, and sponges on the completion of the work, and left clean and perfect before delivery to the trustees.

Brick Work Back up the first two courses of granite and marble as shown with hard North River brick, laid in Meier's cement mortar as already described.

A plaster model of the bronze base to flagpole, and letters, wreaths, etc., will be submitted to the architects for their approval, *Bronze* the modeller to be selected by the architects, and the *Work* model when approved must be carried out in the execution of the work to their entire satisfaction.

Bronze metal to be composed of 90% copper and 10% tin alloy, ⅛ths of which is to be all tin. The base to be made in separate rings, each with flange bearings at the moldings shown to permit of the sway of the pole ; the bottom ring to be secured to the granite cap of pedestal by bronze expansion bolts through flanges cast on the ring for that purpose, or bronze knees. On the top ring provide proper flashing let into the pole, and cover the upper surface of top ring. The whole bronze work to be finished a natural bronze color or oxidized as will be directed by the architects, and be well lacquered before setting.

The letters, wreaths, clasp, and medal will all be of bronze metal, in accordance with the details of same, provided with pins on the backs for securing to face of marble panels. The drilling of the marble for these letters to be done in the most careful manner so that the holes will not be seen after the letters have been put in place, all to be secured with proper cement and cleaned off and left perfect.

A model of the eagle and ball will be made and submitted to the architects for their approval, and the work will be carried out in *Copper Eagle and Ball* accordance therewith with twenty oz. copper. The workmanship to be of the most artistic kind, to be properly mounted on bronze or copper standard, let into and secured to the top of flagpole. The molded capping to the top of pole will be of 20 oz. copper as per detail, all to be finished on surface as directed by the architects.

The flagpole will be of white pine, free from sap, shakes, and all other defects, 18 inches diameter at the butt, 7½ inches diameter *Flagpole* at the top, and not less than 90 feet long, to be dressed round and tapering and well smoothed with sandpaper, ready for painting.

The portion of the flagpole imbedded in the iron shoe, concrete, and masonry to receive two good coats of waterproof asphaltic cement before setting, the remainder of the pole to be painted four coats of white lead and oil, flat finish, or colored as may be decided by the architects.

The pole to be provided with solid bronze pulley block at top, properly secured there, and bronze cleats at bottom with best quality Manila halyards of sufficient size and length.

LIST OF MEMBERS OF LAFAYETTE POST WHO SUBSCRIBED FOR THE PEDESTAL, STAFF, AND FLAGS

ATWOOD, C. G.
ADAMS, G. E.
AGENS, F. G.
ADAMS, H. H.
AMMON, JOHN H.

BACH, JAMES B.
BUTTERFIELD, DANIEL
BARNES, A. C.
BENTON, C. A.
BLANCHARD, JAS. A.
BAKEWELL, A. C.
BROWER, BLOOMFIELD
BRIGGS, JOHN
BRADY, OWEN J.
BARNES, EDWARD F.
BLACKGROVE, J. F.
BOSTROEM, A.
BURGOYNE, THEO.
BRITTON, EUGENE
BANTA, WM.
BLAKE, ASA S.
BLASCHECK, JOSEPH
BOLANDER, W. H.

BRINCKERHOFF, G. G.
BUEK, CHAS.
BURTIS, J. S.
BRACKETT, L. C.
BARTLETT, H. T.
BENSON, JAMES
BROWN, WILBUR F.
BOLITHO, EDWIN
BENNETT, EZRA W.
BURRELL, J. P.
BROWN, CHAS. E.
BEYEA, DR. J. L.
BENEDICT, C. A.
BANKS, JOSEPH E.
BUTLER, G. B.
BUTLER, E. M.
BUTLER, H. P.
BADGER, W. W.
BRUNDAGE, M. T.
BARKER, EDWARD
BARNES, F. E.
BRADY, JAS. W.
BROOKS, F. W.
BRAMAN, JOS. B.

BARRON, JOHN C.
BENT, F. E.
BEACH, DENNIS
BARGER, F. C.
BONTECOU, A. F.
BLOOMINGDALE, LYMAN G.
BUSSEY, CYRUS

CHASE, C. W.
COOKE, G. T.
COPP, WM. A.
CONKLIN, EUGENE H.
COGSWELL, W. S.
CHEROUNY, H. W.
CONNOR, E. S.
CHURCH, H. I.
CURTIS, E. W.
COON, CHAS. H.
CLANCY, JOHN J.
CHAPMAN, J. H.
CLARK, H. O.
CONROW, W. E.
CONROW, THEO.
CANFIELD, C. T.
CROMWELL, GEO.
CURTIS, G. M.
COLLIS, C. H. T.
COFFIN, GEO. H.
CONNELL, W. H.
CALLENDER, W. E.
CLIFFORD, T. B.
CLARKE, L. D.
COBURN, C. M.
CONWAY, J. F.
CLEARMAN, L. L. S.

CASSE, A. J.
COLGATE, JOHN H.
CONTERNO, L.
COWEN, GEO. W.
CUDNER, A. M.
CARHART, JAS. L.
CARMAN, C. Q.
CONNICK, A. J.
COIT, GEO. M.
CASE, GEO. W.
COOPER, J. G.
COOK, JOHN H.

DARLING, W. L.
DAVIS, H. M.
DENNETT, A. W.
DINGMAN, JOHN H.
DUNLAP, G. E.
DEVOE, ISAAC N.
DUSENBERRY, O. W.
DICK, W. B.
DICKINSON, E. B.
DODGE, F. S.
DUNCAN, J. M.
DART, EDWARD
DORE, JOSEPH

EVERTS, DANIEL T.
EDGAR, GEORGE P.
EVANS, L. D.
ELLSWORTH, WM.
EVANS, R. D.
ERNST, WM. M.
EVERSON, CHAS.
EVERSON, W. H.

FOSTER, FRED.
FORDHAM, E. H.
FRANCIS, JOHN H.
FREE, SAMUEL E.
FIELD, R. M., JR.
FRANCIS, A. T.
FLINT, H.
FLYNN, JAMES
FACKNER, EDWARD
FISHER, H. C.
FUNSTON, HUGH M.

GIBBS, T. K.
GREENE, R. H.
GREELEY, A. W.
GARDINER, J. G.
GEROW, J. F.
GRADY, J. H.
GILLEN, D. J.
GREVES, JAMES S.
GILLIS, C. J.
GULAGER, P. D.
GOULD, R. S.
GREENE, A. P.
GALLATIN, FREDERIC
GOODRIDGE, L. O.

HATCH, W. A.
HOMER, C. F.
HENDRICKS, E.
HOOK, S. MERRITT
HADDOCK, WASH'N M.
HECKSCHER, JOHN G.
HYDE, J. B.
HART, LUCIUS

HAMBLER, W. H.
HOPPER, J. C.
HEMMING, JOHN J.
HALL, ERNEST
HALL, A. B.
HILLIARD, J. P.
HAYS, BENJ. J.
HOWLETT, H. J.
HEDENBERG, G. B.
HOTCHKISS, H. L.
HUMMEL, CHAS. C.
HOYT, A. B.
HANKS, HORACE T.
HAMILTON, JOHN
HOWE, S. O.
HERKNER, HENRY F.
HOLLY, HENRY H.
HALL, H. B.
HABERMAN, SIMON
HOWELL, WM. P.
HULL, JOHN H.

JONES, G. W.
JOHNSON, DANIEL H.
JACKSON, W. H.
JOHNSON, R. C.
JONES, MEREDITH L.
JACKSON, E. G.
JAHN, GUSTAVE A.
JAQUES, WASH. L.
JOHNSON, B. S.
JONES, FRANK

KAMPING, J. A.
KEMP, JOHN H.

KENDALL, GEO. M.
KENNEDY, D. T.
KARLEN, A. T.
KELLY, W. J.
KNIGHT, G. N.
KANE, CHAS. W.
KILMER, GEO. L.

LITTLE, JOSEPH J.
LOWERRE, CHAS. H.
LOVELAND, FRANK C.
LODER, GEO. S.
LEMON, W. H.
LEWIS, JOHN N.
LENT, W. H.
LITTLE, JAS. K.
LEWIS, JAMES F.
LITTLE, E.
LAMBERT, WM.
LOWERRE, THOS. H.
LOTT, GEO. G.
LONG, J. C.
LEALE, CHARLES A.
LIBBY, OLIVER
LIVERMORE, FRANK
LAWRENCE, JOHN
LELAND, FRANCIS L.
LOWRY, A. M.
LUDOVICI, JULIUS

McINDOE, P. W.
McCABE, R. T.
McDONALD, J. M.
McMURRAY, R. K.
MILLS, A. G.

MARTIN, H. P.
MORAN, D. C.
MARLOR, H. S.
MEADE, R. W.
MARVIN, A. S.
MORGAN, T. J.
MURRAY, JOSEPH
MILLER, HENRY
MOTT, J. O.
MILLETT, G. S.
MORRIS, FORDHAM
MINGAY, E. B.
MITCHELL, H. W.
MORISON, JAMES J.
MORRISON, R. A.
MORISON, FRED. S.
MARX, DAVID
MOUTOUX, W. E.
MALEES, J. H.
MARLOR, GEO. W.
MURPHY, P. H.
MITCHELL, W. H.

NUGENT, ROBT.
NOE, H. M.
NORRIS, W. L.
NELSON, A.
NORTON, E. N.

OAKES, F. J.
OLCOTT, E. R.
OGDEN, W. B.

PIERSON, J. FRED.
PINKNEY, FRED. H.

PHELPS, H. P.
PERKINS, GEO. F.
PARKINSON, W. B.
PIERSON, H. L.
PROCTOR, WM.
PRIDE, A. H.
PIERCE, L. K.
PERKINS, R. F.
PANCOAST, G. W.
PHELPS, D. F.
PETERSEN, OTTO L.
PLUMMER, J. F.

RANSOM, RASTUS S.
ROSE, DANA A.
RIGGS, GEO. S.
RENNE, D. F.
RICHARDS, T. A.
RATHBONE, R. C.
RAEFLE, MAX G.
RIBLET, W. H.
REGAN, JAMES
ROGERS, W. E.
ROSEDALE, W. V. N.
RICHARDSON, M. H.
ROAKE, JOHN S.
ROBERTS, J. C.
ROBBINS, GEO. W.

SHEPARD, W. E.
SALISBURY, RICHARD L.
SHADE, CHAS. E.
STIEGLITZ, EDWARD
SCOTT, W. A.
SWINNEY, E. G.

SHOEMAKER, H. F.
SETON, WM.
SNYDER, W. J.
SCHEUER, ADOLPH
SIMMONS, H. E.
ST. JOHN, H. W.
SEWARD, REV. S. S.
SAXTON, J. C.
SMITHWICK, J. G.
SUTHERLAND, M. A.
STARR, W. E.
SMITH, GRANVILLE B.
SILL, GEO. W.
STOKES, GEO. W.
SMITH, HENRY A.
SCHOONMAKER, J. S.
SIMPSON, WM.
SEWARD, WM.
SMITH, GEO. W.
STEELE, A. H.
SHEPHERD, CHAS. H. B.
SMITH, RODNEY
SONNENBERG, CHARLES
SMITH, H. COLE
SERRELL, E. W.
STEDMAN, F. B.
STARRING, F. A.
SCOTT, G. D.

TANDY, C. W.
THOMAS, SAM'L
THAYER, H. W.
THOMSON, P. M.
TAYLOR, G. C.
THORP, FRANK

TERRY, JOHN D.
TUCKERMAN, E. G.
THAIN, ALEX.
TUTHILL, GEO.
THOMPSON, JERE S.
TOPPING, C. W.
TUTHILL, H. S.
THORNE, T. A.
TOBIAS, J. M.
TRENOR, H. H.
TOWN, F. E.

UTTER, DR. F. A.
ULMAN, H. CHARLES

VOUTE, J. OSCAR
VAN SICLEN, H. K.
VAN WINKLE, E. B.
VALK, FRANCIS
VILLEPLAIT, A. B.
VAN BENSCHOTEN, E. W.
VASSAR, R. G.
VAIL, G. F.
VAN VLECK, A. K.
VOSBURGH, A.

WHITFIELD, F. A.
WRIGHT, D. F.

WALLING, J. H.
WILLIAMS, EDGAR
WEEBER, WM.
WOTHERSPOON, H. H.
WYMAN, J. C.
WRAY, A. H.
WESSELLS, C. H.
WALKER, J. Q. A.
WICKHAM, D. O.
WOLFE, H. G.
WOOD, E. E.
WILSON, JOHN M.
WYCKOFF, ALBERT T.
WRIGHT, C. J.
WELLS, I. J.
WALLACE, WM.
WHITE, HENRY K.
WELLMAN, W. P.
WARE, R. F.
WAGNER, FRED C.
WEBB, HENRY
WEBB, ALEX. S.
WOOD, WILBUR FISKE
WASHBURN, GEO. W.
WATTSON, E. D.
WHITMAN, GEORGE A.

YORK, J. F.

HALL, W. P.   SABIN, N. H.   TOWS, C. D.

ORIGIN OF FLAG PRESENTATION TO EDUCATIONAL INSTITUTIONS

Previous to the year 1888 the flying of the United States flag over educational institutions, or the display of them within the buildings, was almost unknown. There had been a few instances of presenting them to public schools in the city of New York, which practice was inaugurated by Mr. DeWitt C. Ward, a school trustee of the —— Ward, who by his individual effort had secured flags for perhaps a half dozen schools, and publicly presenting them with patriotic addresses in the assembly rooms, when the scholars were gathered to formally receive them. On one of these occasions Comrade Charles F. Homer was present, and being impressed with the educational value of such a movement, if made general and impressive, in inculcating a spirit of patriotism and reverence for the emblem which had cost so much in lives and money to preserve, especially among the children of foreign parentage whose home education did not tend in that direction, he brought the inspiration to an encampment of Lafayette Post, and in well-chosen words related his experience, and prophesied the benefit to the country should such a movement inspire a general following, and an example set by the Post become universal throughout the land. Feeling the pulse of the comrades of the Post, he was convinced of the popularity of such an inauguration, and offered the following resolution:

" That Lafayette Post present to the College of the City of New York a stand of colors, and permission be granted to start a subscription list for said purpose, and that the Commander appoint a committee of five to provide and make proper arrangements for the presentation."

This was May 4, 1888.

On June 8th following a national silk flag, mounted on a staff, suitably engraved, was presented to the College in the Academy of Music in the presence of the trustees, faculty, and students, and a large assembly of the families and friends of all interested.

The ceremonies were elaborate and impressive, beginning with a prayer by the Rev. S. S. Seward, chaplain of the Post, followed by the presentation address of late Commander Floyd Clarkson, now numbered with the host encamping on the eternal plains of Everlasting Peace. The acceptance was by Gen. Alexander S. Webb, President of the College, who soon after united with the Post and became a comrade of the Grand Army of the Republic. The Hon. J. Edward Simmons, chairman of the Board of Trustees; the Rev. Dr. John R. Paxton, and Gen. Cyrus Bussey made stirring addresses, which were received with cheers and applause.

Thus began the spirited patriotic work of Lafayette Post, which has grown with a rapidity far beyond the most sanguine hopes, until the flag floats, to-day, over nearly every college and school throughout the broad land, until upon the statute books of many States may be read the law compelling public schools to float the flag of liberty during their session, and making it a penal offence to those in control to disobey the enactment.

Between June, 1888, and May, 1898, the Post has donated many flags, and presented them with more or less ceremony in different places, besides in other ways showing a patriotic fervor and a desire to inculcate a spirit of reverence for heroic merit and national service.

OCCASIONS OF FLAG PRESENTATION BY LAFAYETTE POST OTHER THAN TO COLUMBIA COLLEGE

October 18, 1889

To Lafayette Camp, No. 140, Sons of Veterans, Division of New York.

Presentation address by Gen. William T. Sherman.

Acceptance by Edward Trenchard, Captain of the Camp.

June 6, 1890

To Primary School No. 87.

Presentation address by General Viele, Commander of Post.

October 14, 1890

To Packer Collegiate and Polytechnic Institutes of Brooklyn, N. Y., at the Brooklyn Academy of Music, by comrades of the Post residing in Brooklyn.

Introduction by Gen. Henry W. Slocum.

Prayer by Rev. Charles H. Hall, D.D.

Presentation address by Commander Egbert L. Viele.

Acceptance for Polytechnic by President David H. Cochran, LL.D.; for Packer by President Truman J. Backus, LL.D.

Addresses by Gen. William T. Sherman and Hon. Seth Low.

May 20, 1893

Stand of colors to Girard College, Philadelphia, on birthday of Founder Stephen Girard.

Presentation by Comrade Charles H. T. Collis.

Acceptance by Professor A. H. Felteroy, President of College.

Address by Hon. Charles Emory Smith, ex-United States Minister to Russia.

June 14, 1895

To Havemeyer School, Greenwich, Conn.

September 28, 1895

To Grammar School at Greensburgh, near Elmsford, N. Y.

December 26, 1895

To cadets of St. Paul Church, New York City.

March 9, 1897

To Rhinelander School, 350 East Eighty-eighth Street, New York City. Miss Margaret P. Pascal, principal.

Presentation address by Commander Josiah C. Long.

Acceptance by Master Hass of the School Battalion.

February 11, 1898

To Grammar School No. 23, New York City.

Lafayette Post and the Flag

February 22, 1898

Four guidons to Baron de Hirsch English Day School at the Educational Alliance, Jefferson Street and East Broadway.

Presentation address by Comrade George W. Jones.

Acceptance by a Russian girl pupil five years old.

SOME OTHER PATRIOTIC WORK

1893

Resolutions on Military Instruction in Public Schools, by Comrade E. L. Zalinski, adopted by Twenty-seventh National Encampment, G. A. R., at Indianapolis, Ind.

1897–1898

Support of a class in elementary civics under the charge of Miss Margaret P. Pascal.

Spring and Summer, 1898

A committee of this Post, appointed by the Post to raise volunteers for the war with Spain, enrolled more than 7,000 men, and placed nearly 3,000 in the volunteer service and about 800 in the regular army, receiving the commendation of the President of the United States, Secretary of War, and the Adjutant-General of the Army.*

May 30, 1898

Dedication of memorial tablet erected by the Post at Brinckerhoff, N. Y., in honor of Maj.-Gen. Marquis de

---

* The Post, by resolution adopted April 7th, ordered that the report of the committee having this work in charge should be printed in this volume. It will be found on pages 115 to 121.

Lafayette, and presented to Melzingah Chapter, Daughters of American Revolution.

Presentation address by Commander Daniel Butterfield.

Acceptance by Mrs. Ver Planck.

Address by Gen. Henry E. Tremaine.

December, 1898

Six hundred bunting flags, four feet by six, were sent to Porto Rico in charge of Junior Vice-Commander Bakewell under orders of the Adjutant-General of the State of New York and with the approval and commendation of the United States Government, and were distributed to the various schools and educational institutions of the island to the delight of the authorities, military and civil, and of the teachers and scholars.

January 27, 1899

Bunting flag, standard size, trimmed with yellow silk fringe and cord and tassels, mounted on a nine-foot ash pole, was presented to Grammar School No. 85, 138th Street, between Willis and Brooke Avenues.

February 22, 1899

A large flag was presented by Past Commander Long, for the Post, to the St. Luke's Boys' Club of the Protestant Episcopal Church of Brooklyn.

FINAL REPORT

OF

COMMITTEE APPOINTED BY LAFAYETTE POST TO RECRUIT VOLUNTEERS FOR THE WAR WITH SPAIN.

NEW YORK, *April* 7, 1899.

COMMANDER AND COMRADES :

The war with Spain having definitely ended by the ratification of the treaty of peace on the part of Spain, your Committee begs to submit this final report and to ask its discharge.

The work of the Committee has been fully reported from time to time at the encampments of the Post, but it is deemed fitting to submit here a brief review of its proceedings.

The undertaking had its inception in a suggestion informally made by the then Commander of the Post, Major-General Daniel Butterfield, about six weeks before the declaration of war. This suggestion was followed by the issue of a confidential circular by Commander Butterfield, under date of March 25, 1898, pointing out the opportunity and the duty of members of the Post to aid the Government by their experience, influence, and active work in raising a model regiment to enter the service in the event of the actual outbreak of war. A copy of this circular letter of March 25, 1898, also copies of all subsequent printed and written letters, and of all official papers issued by the Committee, together with the record of proceedings of the Committee, accompany this report.

The initial official action taken by the Post itself is shown by the resolution unanimously adopted by a rising vote of all comrades present at the encampment of April 15, 1898, and here reproduced in full:

"*Resolved*, That Lafayette Post, No. 140, Department of New York, Grand Army of the Republic, in regular encampment assembled, hereby endorses the patriotic project to form a Lafayette Post Regiment, as outlined by the circular letter of Commander Daniel Butterfield under date of March 25, 1898, and Post Order No. 7, and pledges its support thereto.

"*Resolved*, further, That Commander Butterfield be, and he is hereby, authorized and requested to appoint a committee, with power, to have charge of the details of raising and organizing such regiment."

The original plan was to recruit and fully equip a regiment to be officered by members of Lafayette Post and Regular Army officers, the rank and file to consist of sons of members of the Post, and of other picked men, all of whom would be willing to serve for the war, whatever might be its duration.

Due, however, to the circumstance that the Government had been persuaded to give to the National Guard of the States the preference in filling the calls for volunteers, it became impossible to procure the acceptance of a distinctively Lafayette Post Regiment, although strenuous and unremitting efforts to that end were made, both with the Federal and State authorities—Commander Butterfield especially having made many trips to Washington and to Albany to accomplish this object.

Notwithstanding the impossibility, for the reason stated, of giving effect to the original plan, the initial work of the Committee had been so thoroughly and vigorously prosecuted, and the interest aroused therein having been so widespread that thousands of young men, eager to serve their country on the lines indicated by your Committee, had responded to our call, it was determined to broaden the work of the Committee, and to make such work of value to the Government in all possible directions, by securing the enlistment of the men thus enrolled, in the different National Guard Regiments of the State and in the Regular Army and Navy.

This extension of the original work allotted to the Committee was duly reported to the Post, and received its enthusiastic and unanimous approval.

While we would not be justified in occupying space here with statistics, which will be found in full in the papers filed with this report, it might be stated briefly that more than 7,000 men were enrolled for service in the war by your Committee, and that more than half of this number were placed in the service in the National Guard and in the Regular Army and Navy of the United States.

The work thus undertaken and accomplished by the Post through the medium of your Committee, received the unqualified endorsement, not alone of Federal and

State authorities, but also of the Commander-in-Chief of the Grand Army of the Republic, the Commander of the Department of New York, and of the comrades generally.

Of the many testimonials communicated to the Post or to the Committee and filed with this report, perhaps the following brief extract from the letter of the Adjutant-General of the Army, written December 15, 1898, long after the close of active operations, will sufficiently indicate the appreciation of the work accomplished, for no other officer in the service had such opportunity to judge of the extent and value of such work as the Adjutant-General of the Army, who then said in an official letter to Commander Butterfield: " Please say to Lafayette Post that its work in support of the Government during the war with Spain was second to that of no other organization in the country, and so far as I am able to speak for the War Department, I thank you, each and every one of you."

This patriotic work—thus originating in the undertaking to raise a Lafayette Post Regiment, and extending on broader lines for the reasons herein assigned—was by no means selfishly prosecuted for the glory and credit of Lafayette Post alone, but, at an early stage of the Committee's work, by a carefully prepared circular letter, dated April 11, 1898, the prosecution of similar work by all other Grand Army Posts was urged, and the great value to the Government of such a service by the veterans of the Civil War was plainly pointed out. In New York State, and in other States as well, work on similar lines was undertaken by comrades of the Grand Army, and, in our own State, we received valuable assistance from comrades, especially at Port Jervis, Oswego, Nyack, Utica, Warsaw, Rochester, Albany, and other towns in the interior of the State.

The aid rendered the Committee by different individuals and organizations has been duly acknowledged by resolutions of thanks adopted and by testimonials awarded by vote of the Post.

The large number of members of the Post who actively aided the Committee in its work have found their adequate reward in the opportunity afforded them, and of which they eagerly availed themselves, to participate in this self-denying and patriotic service.

Your Committee deems it appropriate, however, to here restate the specific service rendered by some of our patriotic citizens, although in every case such service has been duly acknowledged by a Post resolution:

Hon. Samuel A. Blatchford, free use of entire building northeast corner Fourteenth Street and Fifth Avenue for an armory and recruiting station.

Home Life Insurance Company, spacious and admirably located offices for the use of the Committee and its clerical staff.

Hon. Augustus A. Low, of Brooklyn, use of a large and appropriate office for recruiting headquarters in that city.

Messrs. D. O. Mills and Ogden Mills, use of store in Mills Hotel No. 1 for recruiting station.

Also a number of other citizens and members of the Post in New York, Brooklyn, and in cities in the interior of the State, granted the use of appropriate rooms or offices, free of charge, as recruiting stations. In all cases such assistance was suitably acknowledged.

In addition we were at different times granted the use of the Seventh, Ninth, and Twelfth Regiment Armories for parade and inspection of our volunteers.

At the very outset of our undertaking, in response to an appeal by Commander Butterfield, the Hon. Cornelius N. Bliss, then Secretary of the Interior, very promptly and cordially tendered the gift of 7,000 yards of cloth to make uniforms.

Shortly thereafter Lyman G. Bloomingdale, a comrade of this Post, offered, on behalf of his firm, to make up such cloth into uniforms for the Lafayette Post Regiment, and also granted the use of a spacious room in their building as a recruiting headquarters.

Mr. Louis Stern, on behalf of Messrs. Stern Brothers, offered to provide uniforms for an entire regiment, and

Mr. Frederick Gallatin, a comrade of this Post, made a similar offer.

It would be impossible to give within the limits of this report the names of all the patriotic citizens who in various ways tendered their aid in furtherance of our patriotic work.

The expenses of the Committee amounted to many thousand dollars, and were met by the voluntary contributions of members of the Post, with the exception of one contribution of one hundred dollars. Several members of the Post, notably the Secretary of the Committee, freely gave all of their time to the work of the Committee.

Lafayette Post has the distinction of all organizations

of the country of being the very first to take practical steps to render substantial aid to the Government in the then existing crisis, and while, due to the circumstance set forth in this report, and with which all members of the Post are familiar, it failed to accomplish its original object of placing its own regiment in the field, it did bear a useful and honorable part, and conspicuously exemplified the crowning principle of our order, " Loyalty."

Respectfully submitted,

By order of the Committee,

A. G. MILLS,

Chairman.

A. C. BAKEWELL,

Secretary.

www.ingramcontent.com/pod-product-compliance
Lightning Source LLC
Chambersburg PA
CBHW030631270326
41927CB00007B/1398